WEEK OF:									
GOALS:		MINUTES							
TOPIC	DESCRIPTION	Sun	Mon	Tue	Wed	Thu	Fri	Sat
CHORDS								
SCALES								
ARPEGGIOS								
SONGS								
LICKS/RIFFS								
OTHER								

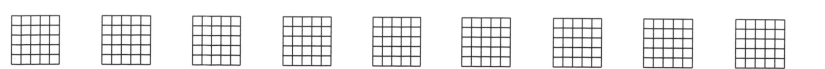

WEEK OF:									
GOALS:		MINUTES							
TOPIC	DESCRIPTION	Sun	Mon	Tue	Wed	Thu	Fri	Sat
CHORDS								
SCALES								
ARPEGGIOS								
SONGS								
LICKS/RIFFS								
OTHER								

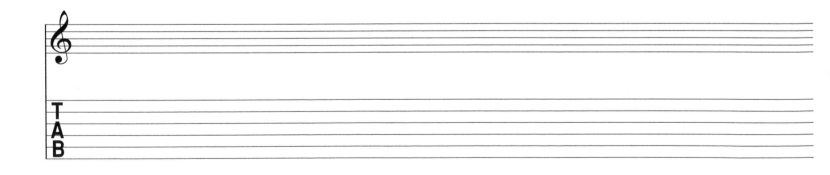

WEEK OF:		MINUTES						
GOALS:		Sun	Mon	Tue	Wed	Thu	Fri	Sat
TOPIC	DESCRIPTION	Sun	Mon	Tue	Wed	Thu	Fri	Sat
CHORDS								
SCALES								
ARPEGGIOS								
SONGS								
LICKS/RIFFS								
OTHER								

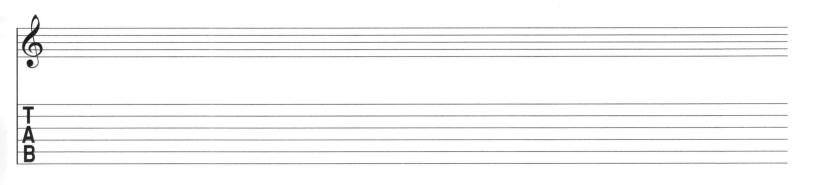

WEEK OF:									
GOALS:			MINUTES						
TOPIC	DESCRIPTION	Sun	Mon	Tue	Wed	Thu	Fri	Sat	
CHORDS									
SCALES									
ARPEGGIOS									
SONGS									
LICKS/RIFFS									
OTHER									

WEEK OF:										
GOALS:			MINUTES							
TOPIC	DESCRIPTION		Sun	Mon	Tue	Wed	Thu	Fri	Sat	
CHORDS										
SCALES										
ARPEGGIOS										
SONGS										
LICKS/RIFFS										
OTHER										

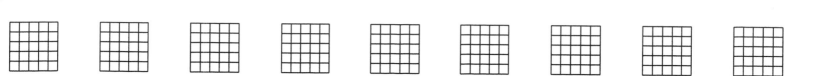

WEEK OF:								
GOALS:		MINUTES						
TOPIC	DESCRIPTION	Sun	Mon	Tue	Wed	Thu	Fri	Sat
CHORDS								
SCALES								
ARPEGGIOS								
SONGS								
LICKS/RIFFS								
OTHER								

WEEK OF:										
GOALS:			MINUTES							
TOPIC	DESCRIPTION		Sun	Mon	Tue	Wed	Thu	Fri	Sat	
CHORDS										
SCALES										
ARPEGGIOS										
SONGS										
LICKS/RIFFS										
OTHER										

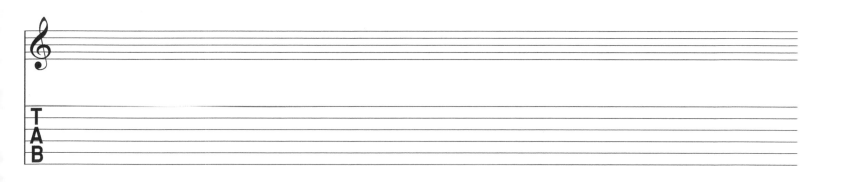

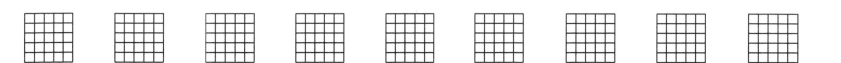

WEEK OF:										
GOALS:			MINUTES							
TOPIC	DESCRIPTION		Sun	Mon	Tue	Wed	Thu	Fri	Sat	
CHORDS										
SCALES										
ARPEGGIOS										
SONGS										
LICKS/RIFFS										
OTHER										

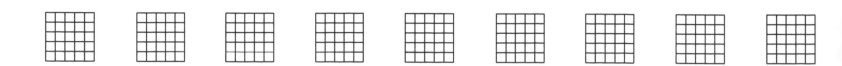

WEEK OF:		MINUTES						
GOALS:		Sun	Mon	Tue	Wed	Thu	Fri	Sat
TOPIC	DESCRIPTION	Sun	Mon	Tue	Wed	Thu	Fri	Sat
CHORDS								
SCALES								
ARPEGGIOS								
SONGS								
LICKS/RIFFS								
OTHER								

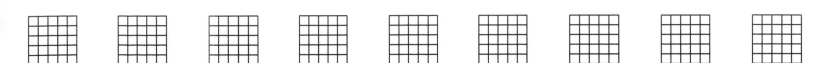

WEEK OF:									
GOALS:		MINUTES							
TOPIC	DESCRIPTION	Sun	Mon	Tue	Wed	Thu	Fri	Sat
CHORDS								
SCALES								
ARPEGGIOS								
SONGS								
LICKS/RIFFS								
OTHER								

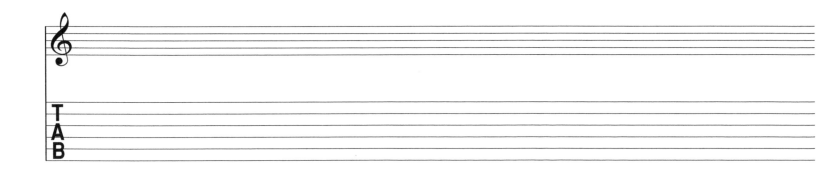

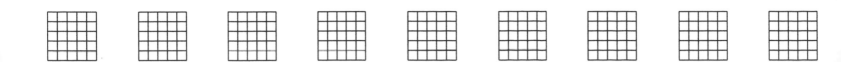

WEEK OF:									
GOALS:			MINUTES						
TOPIC	DESCRIPTION		Sun	Mon	Tue	Wed	Thu	Fri	Sat
CHORDS									
SCALES									
ARPEGGIOS									
SONGS									
LICKS/RIFFS									
OTHER									

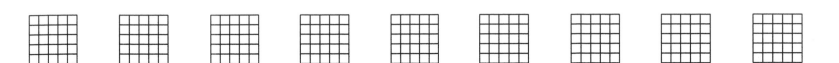

WEEK OF:								
GOALS:		MINUTES						
TOPIC	DESCRIPTION	Sun	Mon	Tue	Wed	Thu	Fri	Sat
CHORDS								
SCALES								
ARPEGGIOS								
SONGS								
LICKS/RIFFS								
OTHER								

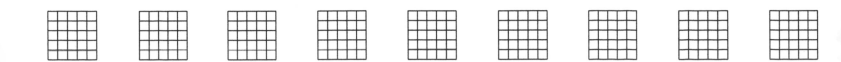

WEEK OF:									
GOALS:			MINUTES						
TOPIC	DESCRIPTION	Sun	Mon	Tue	Wed	Thu	Fri	Sat
CHORDS								
SCALES								
ARPEGGIOS								
SONGS								
LICKS/RIFFS								
OTHER								

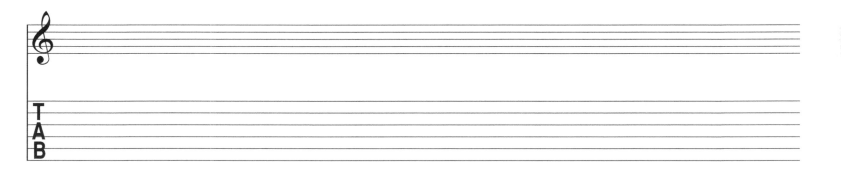

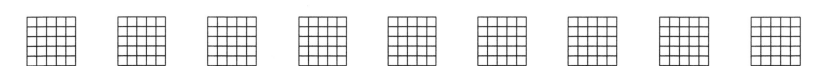

WEEK OF:								
GOALS:		MINUTES						
TOPIC	DESCRIPTION	Sun	Mon	Tue	Wed	Thu	Fri	Sat
CHORDS								
SCALES								
ARPEGGIOS								
SONGS								
LICKS/RIFFS								
OTHER								

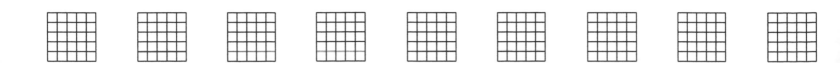

WEEK OF:									
GOALS:		MINUTES							
TOPIC	DESCRIPTION	Sun	Mon	Tue	Wed	Thu	Fri	Sat
CHORDS								
SCALES								
ARPEGGIOS								
SONGS								
LICKS/RIFFS								
OTHER								

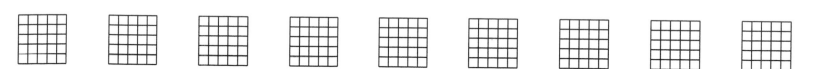

WEEK OF:									
GOALS:			MINUTES						
TOPIC	DESCRIPTION		Sun	Mon	Tue	Wed	Thu	Fri	Sat
CHORDS									
SCALES									
ARPEGGIOS									
SONGS									
LICKS/RIFFS									
OTHER									

TOPIC	DESCRIPTION	MINUTES						
		Sun	Mon	Tue	Wed	Thu	Fri	Sat
CHORDS								
SCALES								
ARPEGGIOS								
SONGS								
LICKS/RIFFS								
OTHER								

WEEK OF:

GOALS:

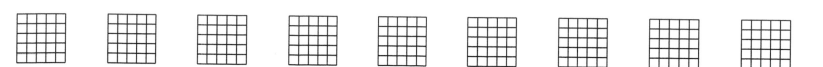

WEEK OF:								
GOALS:		MINUTES						
TOPIC	DESCRIPTION	Sun	Mon	Tue	Wed	Thu	Fri	Sat
CHORDS								
SCALES								
ARPEGGIOS								
SONGS								
LICKS/RIFFS								
OTHER								

WEEK OF:									
GOALS:		MINUTES							
TOPIC	DESCRIPTION	Sun	Mon	Tue	Wed	Thu	Fri	Sat
CHORDS								
SCALES								
ARPEGGIOS								
SONGS								
LICKS/RIFFS								
OTHER								

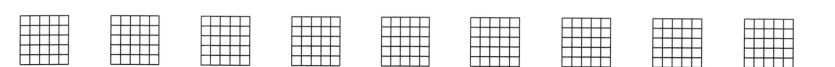

WEEK OF:								
GOALS:		MINUTES						
TOPIC	DESCRIPTION	Sun	Mon	Tue	Wed	Thu	Fri	Sat
CHORDS								
SCALES								
ARPEGGIOS								
SONGS								
LICKS/RIFFS								
OTHER								

TOPIC	DESCRIPTION	MINUTES						
		Sun	Mon	Tue	Wed	Thu	Fri	Sat
CHORDS								
SCALES								
ARPEGGIOS								
SONGS								
LICKS/RIFFS								
OTHER								

WEEK OF:

GOALS:

TOPIC	DESCRIPTION	MINUTES						
WEEK OF:								
GOALS:								
		Sun	Mon	Tue	Wed	Thu	Fri	Sat
CHORDS								
SCALES								
ARPEGGIOS								
SONGS								
LICKS/RIFFS								
OTHER								

WEEK OF:		MINUTES						
GOALS:								
TOPIC	DESCRIPTION	Sun	Mon	Tue	Wed	Thu	Fri	Sat
CHORDS								
SCALES								
ARPEGGIOS								
SONGS								
LICKS/RIFFS								
OTHER								

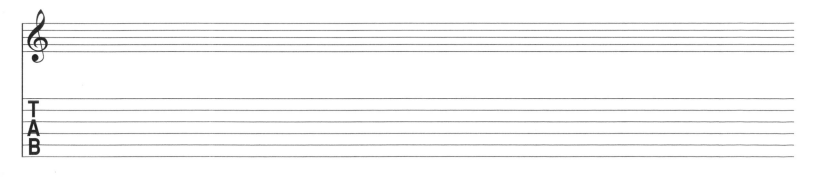

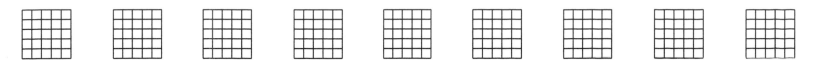

WEEK OF:								
GOALS:				MINUTES				
TOPIC	DESCRIPTION	Sun	Mon	Tue	Wed	Thu	Fri	Sat
CHORDS								
SCALES								
ARPEGGIOS								
SONGS								
LICKS/RIFFS								
OTHER								

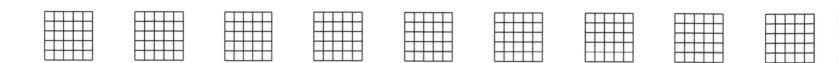

WEEK OF:									
GOALS:			MINUTES						
TOPIC	DESCRIPTION		Sun	Mon	Tue	Wed	Thu	Fri	Sat
CHORDS									
SCALES									
ARPEGGIOS									
SONGS									
LICKS/RIFFS									
OTHER									

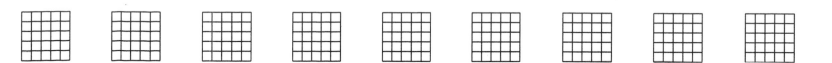

WEEK OF:			MINUTES						
GOALS:			Sun	Mon	Tue	Wed	Thu	Fri	Sat
TOPIC	DESCRIPTION								
CHORDS									
SCALES									
ARPEGGIOS									
SONGS									
LICKS/RIFFS									
OTHER									

WEEK OF:			MINUTES						
GOALS:									
TOPIC	DESCRIPTION	Sun	Mon	Tue	Wed	Thu	Fri	Sat
CHORDS								
SCALES								
ARPEGGIOS								
SONGS								
LICKS/RIFFS								
OTHER								

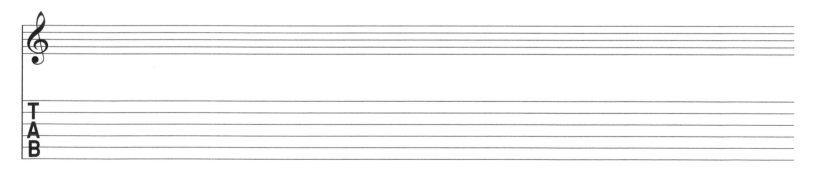

WEEK OF:									
GOALS:			MINUTES						
TOPIC	DESCRIPTION		Sun	Mon	Tue	Wed	Thu	Fri	Sat
CHORDS									
SCALES									
ARPEGGIOS									
SONGS									
LICKS/RIFFS									
OTHER									

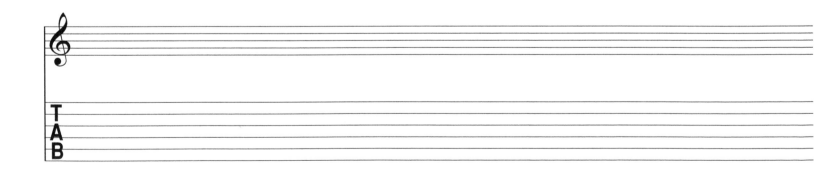

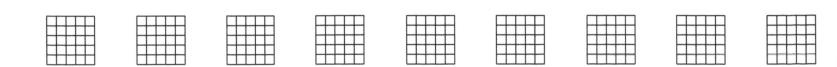

WEEK OF:								
GOALS:		MINUTES						
TOPIC	DESCRIPTION	Sun	Mon	Tue	Wed	Thu	Fri	Sat
CHORDS								
SCALES								
ARPEGGIOS								
SONGS								
LICKS/RIFFS								
OTHER								

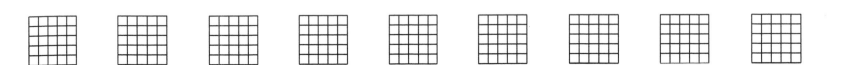

TOPIC	DESCRIPTION	MINUTES						
		Sun	Mon	Tue	Wed	Thu	Fri	Sat
CHORDS								
SCALES								
ARPEGGIOS								
SONGS								
LICKS/RIFFS								
OTHER								

WEEK OF:

GOALS:

WEEK OF:								
GOALS:			MINUTES					
TOPIC	DESCRIPTION	Sun	Mon	Tue	Wed	Thu	Fri	Sat
CHORDS								
SCALES								
ARPEGGIOS								
SONGS								
LICKS/RIFFS								
OTHER								

WEEK OF:								
GOALS:		MINUTES						
TOPIC	DESCRIPTION	Sun	Mon	Tue	Wed	Thu	Fri	Sat
CHORDS								
SCALES								
ARPEGGIOS								
SONGS								
LICKS/RIFFS								
OTHER								

WEEK OF:									
GOALS:		**MINUTES**							
TOPIC	**DESCRIPTION**	Sun	Mon	Tue	Wed	Thu	Fri	Sat	
CHORDS									
SCALES									
ARPEGGIOS									
SONGS									
LICKS/RIFFS									
OTHER									

WEEK OF:								
GOALS:		MINUTES						
TOPIC	DESCRIPTION	Sun	Mon	Tue	Wed	Thu	Fri	Sat
CHORDS								
SCALES								
ARPEGGIOS								
SONGS								
LICKS/RIFFS								
OTHER								

WEEK OF:								
GOALS:		MINUTES						
TOPIC	DESCRIPTION	Sun	Mon	Tue	Wed	Thu	Fri	Sat
CHORDS								
SCALES								
ARPEGGIOS								
SONGS								
LICKS/RIFFS								
OTHER								

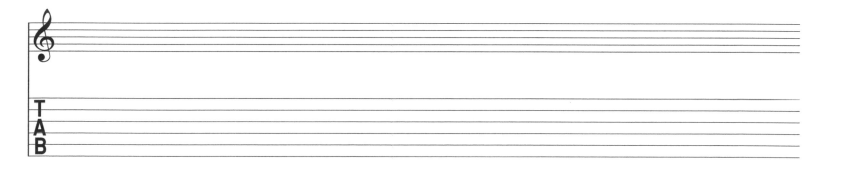

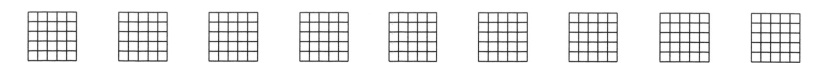

WEEK OF:									
GOALS:		MINUTES							
TOPIC	DESCRIPTION	Sun	Mon	Tue	Wed	Thu	Fri	Sat
CHORDS								
SCALES								
ARPEGGIOS								
SONGS								
LICKS/RIFFS								
OTHER								

WEEK OF:									
GOALS:			MINUTES						
TOPIC	DESCRIPTION		Sun	Mon	Tue	Wed	Thu	Fri	Sat
CHORDS									
SCALES									
ARPEGGIOS									
SONGS									
LICKS/RIFFS									
OTHER									

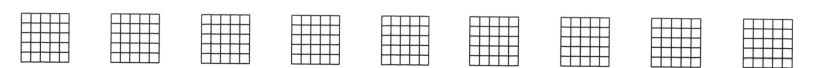

WEEK OF:									
GOALS:			MINUTES						
TOPIC	DESCRIPTION		Sun	Mon	Tue	Wed	Thu	Fri	Sat
CHORDS									
SCALES									
ARPEGGIOS									
SONGS									
LICKS/RIFFS									
OTHER									

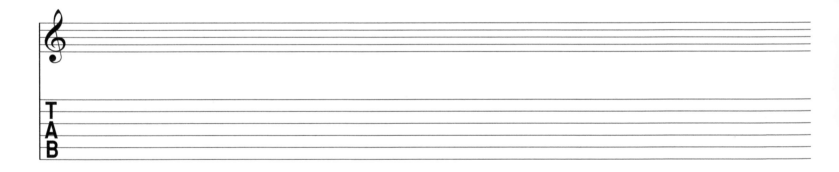

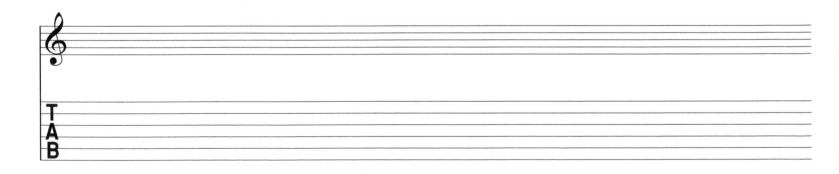

WEEK OF:									
GOALS:			MINUTES						
TOPIC	DESCRIPTION		Sun	Mon	Tue	Wed	Thu	Fri	Sat
CHORDS									
SCALES									
ARPEGGIOS									
SONGS									
LICKS/RIFFS									
OTHER									

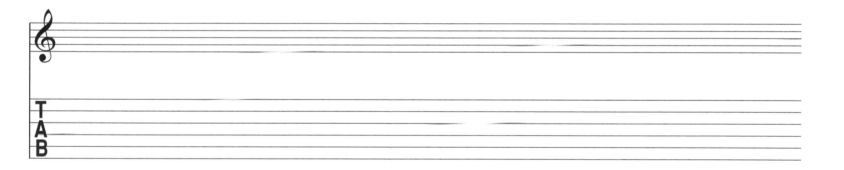

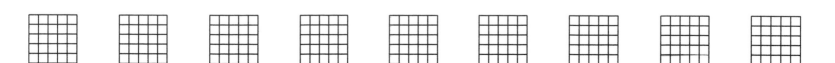

WEEK OF:										
GOALS:				MINUTES						
TOPIC	DESCRIPTION		Sun	Mon	Tue	Wed	Thu	Fri	Sat
CHORDS									
SCALES									
ARPEGGIOS									
SONGS									
LICKS/RIFFS									
OTHER									

WEEK OF:									
GOALS:		MINUTES							
TOPIC	DESCRIPTION	Sun	Mon	Tue	Wed	Thu	Fri	Sat
CHORDS								
SCALES								
ARPEGGIOS								
SONGS								
LICKS/RIFFS								
OTHER								

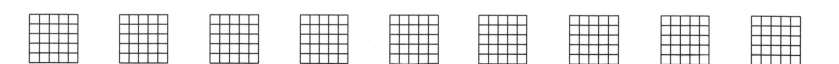

WEEK OF:		MINUTES							
GOALS:									
TOPIC	DESCRIPTION	Sun	Mon	Tue	Wed	Thu	Fri	Sat
CHORDS								
SCALES								
ARPEGGIOS								
SONGS								
LICKS/RIFFS								
OTHER								

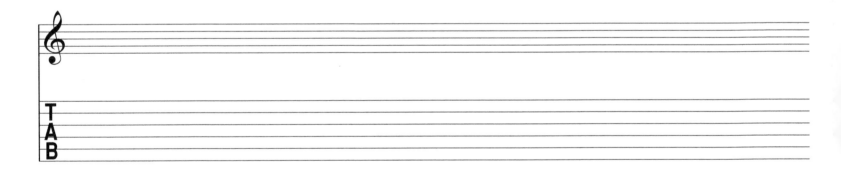

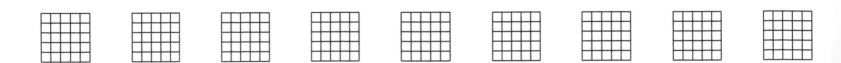

WEEK OF:									
GOALS:				MINUTES					
TOPIC	DESCRIPTION	Sun	Mon	Tue	Wed	Thu	Fri	Sat
CHORDS								
SCALES								
ARPEGGIOS								
SONGS								
LICKS/RIFFS								
OTHER								

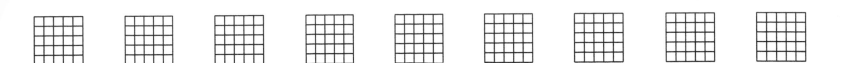

WEEK OF:									
GOALS:			MINUTES						
TOPIC	DESCRIPTION		Sun	Mon	Tue	Wed	Thu	Fri	Sat
CHORDS									
SCALES									
ARPEGGIOS									
SONGS									
LICKS/RIFFS									
OTHER									

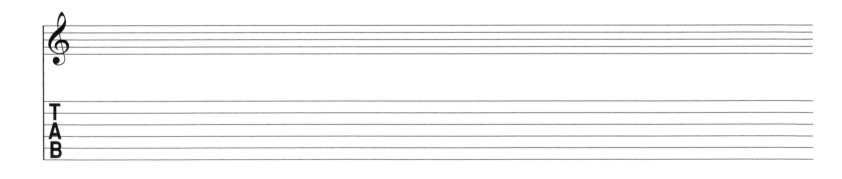

TOPIC	DESCRIPTION	MINUTES						
WEEK OF:								
GOALS:								
		Sun	Mon	Tue	Wed	Thu	Fri	Sat
CHORDS								
SCALES								
ARPEGGIOS								
SONGS								
LICKS/RIFFS								
OTHER								

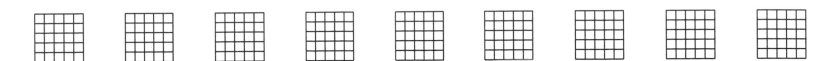

WEEK OF:									
GOALS:		**MINUTES**							
TOPIC	DESCRIPTION	Sun	Mon	Tue	Wed	Thu	Fri	Sat
CHORDS								
SCALES								
ARPEGGIOS								
SONGS								
LICKS/RIFFS								
OTHER								

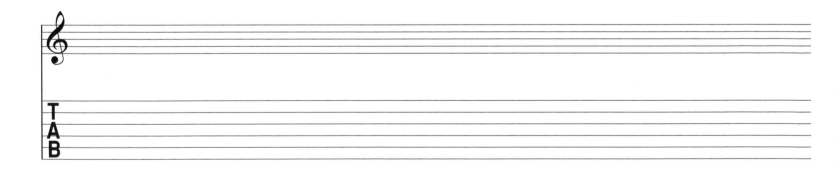

WEEK OF:								
GOALS:		MINUTES						
TOPIC	DESCRIPTION	Sun	Mon	Tue	Wed	Thu	Fri	Sat
CHORDS								
SCALES								
ARPEGGIOS								
SONGS								
LICKS/RIFFS								
OTHER								

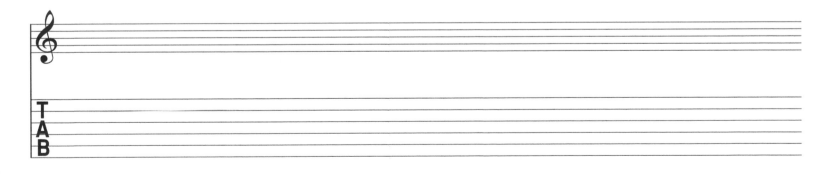

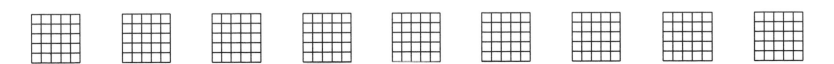

WEEK OF:									
GOALS:		MINUTES							
TOPIC	DESCRIPTION	Sun	Mon	Tue	Wed	Thu	Fri	Sat	
CHORDS									
SCALES									
ARPEGGIOS									
SONGS									
LICKS/RIFFS									
OTHER									

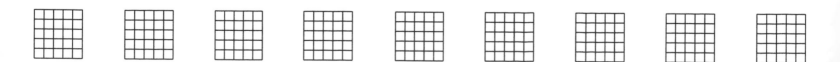

WEEK OF:									
GOALS:		MINUTES							
TOPIC	DESCRIPTION	Sun	Mon	Tue	Wed	Thu	Fri	Sat
CHORDS								
SCALES								
ARPEGGIOS								
SONGS								
LICKS/RIFFS								
OTHER								

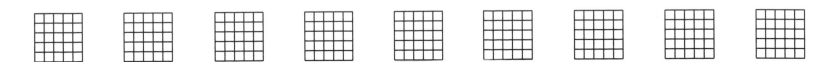

WEEK OF:									
GOALS:			MINUTES						
TOPIC	DESCRIPTION		Sun	Mon	Tue	Wed	Thu	Fri	Sat
CHORDS									
SCALES									
ARPEGGIOS									
SONGS									
LICKS/RIFFS									
OTHER									

WEEK OF:									
GOALS:		MINUTES							
TOPIC	DESCRIPTION	Sun	Mon	Tue	Wed	Thu	Fri	Sat
CHORDS								
SCALES								
ARPEGGIOS								
SONGS								
LICKS/RIFFS								
OTHER								

WEEK OF:									
GOALS:			MINUTES						
TOPIC	DESCRIPTION		Sun	Mon	Tue	Wed	Thu	Fri	Sat
CHORDS									
SCALES									
ARPEGGIOS									
SONGS									
LICKS/RIFFS									
OTHER									

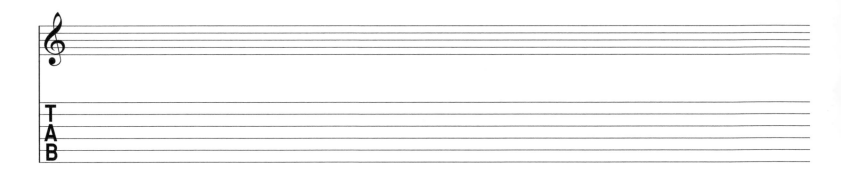

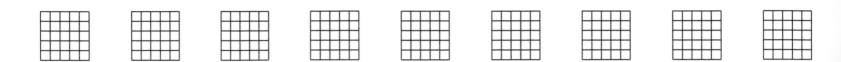

WEEK OF:									
GOALS:		MINUTES							
TOPIC	DESCRIPTION	Sun	Mon	Tue	Wed	Thu	Fri	Sat
CHORDS								
SCALES								
ARPEGGIOS								
SONGS								
LICKS/RIFFS								
OTHER								

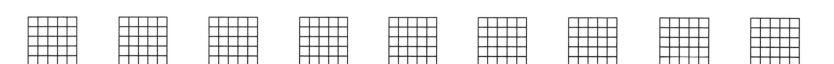

WEEK OF:								
GOALS:		MINUTES						
TOPIC	DESCRIPTION	Sun	Mon	Tue	Wed	Thu	Fri	Sat
CHORDS								
SCALES								
ARPEGGIOS								
SONGS								
LICKS/RIFFS								
OTHER								

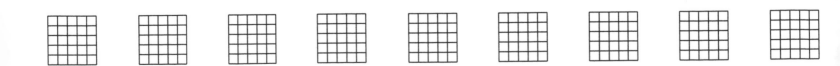

WEEK OF:									
GOALS:		MINUTES							
TOPIC	DESCRIPTION	Sun	Mon	Tue	Wed	Thu	Fri	Sat
CHORDS								
SCALES								
ARPEGGIOS								
SONGS								
LICKS/RIFFS								
OTHER								

WEEK OF:									
GOALS:		MINUTES							
TOPIC	DESCRIPTION	Sun	Mon	Tue	Wed	Thu	Fri	Sat
CHORDS								
SCALES								
ARPEGGIOS								
SONGS								
LICKS/RIFFS								
OTHER								

WEEK OF:									
GOALS:			MINUTES						
TOPIC	DESCRIPTION	Sun	Mon	Tue	Wed	Thu	Fri	Sat
CHORDS								
SCALES								
ARPEGGIOS								
SONGS								
LICKS/RIFFS								
OTHER								

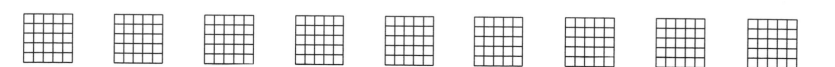

TOPIC	DESCRIPTION	MINUTES						
WEEK OF:								
GOALS:								
		Sun	Mon	Tue	Wed	Thu	Fri	Sat
CHORDS								
SCALES								
ARPEGGIOS								
SONGS								
LICKS/RIFFS								
OTHER								

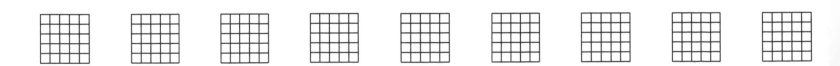

WEEK OF:									
GOALS:		MINUTES							
TOPIC	DESCRIPTION	Sun	Mon	Tue	Wed	Thu	Fri	Sat	
CHORDS									
SCALES									
ARPEGGIOS									
SONGS									
LICKS/RIFFS									
OTHER									

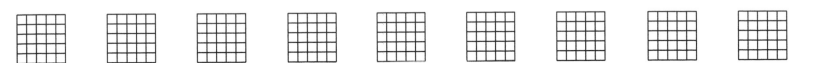

WEEK OF:		MINUTES						
GOALS:								
TOPIC	DESCRIPTION	Sun	Mon	Tue	Wed	Thu	Fri	Sat
CHORDS								
SCALES								
ARPEGGIOS								
SONGS								
LICKS/RIFFS								
OTHER								

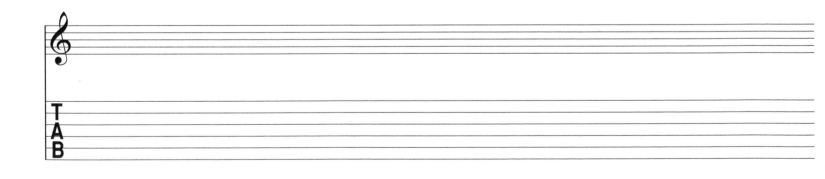

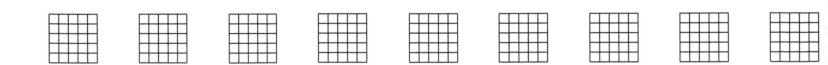

WEEK OF:								
GOALS:		MINUTES						
TOPIC	DESCRIPTION	Sun	Mon	Tue	Wed	Thu	Fri	Sat
CHORDS								
SCALES								
ARPEGGIOS								
SONGS								
LICKS/RIFFS								
OTHER								

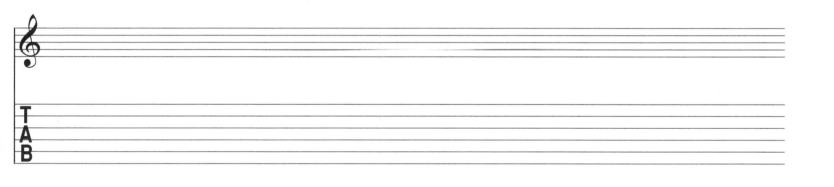

WEEK OF:									
GOALS:		MINUTES							
TOPIC	DESCRIPTION	Sun	Mon	Tue	Wed	Thu	Fri	Sat
CHORDS								
SCALES								
ARPEGGIOS								
SONGS								
LICKS/RIFFS								
OTHER								

WEEK OF:									
GOALS:			MINUTES						
TOPIC	DESCRIPTION	Sun	Mon	Tue	Wed	Thu	Fri	Sat
CHORDS								
SCALES								
ARPEGGIOS								
SONGS								
LICKS/RIFFS								
OTHER								

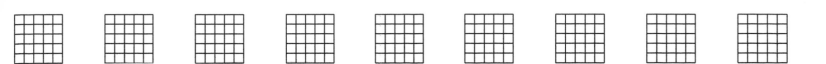

WEEK OF:									
GOALS:			MINUTES						
TOPIC	DESCRIPTION		Sun	Mon	Tue	Wed	Thu	Fri	Sat
CHORDS									
SCALES									
ARPEGGIOS									
SONGS									
LICKS/RIFFS									
OTHER